Text by

Shirley Higginson

Illustrations by

Ranni Pilescu

A Reidmore Book
Fleet Books, Toronto

A Reidmore Book
9115 39 Avenue
Edmonton, Alberta Canada T6E 5Y2

Published by Fleet Publishers
A Division of International Thomson Limited
1410 Birchmount Road
Scarborough, Ontario, Canada M1P 2E7

Canadian Cataloguing in Publication Data

Higginson, Shirley.
Ice Cream Sneakers

ISBN 0-919091-31-8

1. Nonsense-verses, Canadian (English)*
I. Pilescu, Ranni. II. Title.
PS8565.I3913 C811'.54 C82-091259-X PR9199.3.H5313

With love to those who care—
AND to all wart hogs who'd rather be swans.
S.H.

Till Mark, Karin, Erik och dom som kommer
R.P.

It must be awful to be a mouse
When nobody wants you around the house
But if you grow up to be furry and fat
You can stick your tongue out at my cat!

What do think
a banana would say
If a banana could
really talk?
"I have no bones,
I have no stones
And I've never
learned to walk."

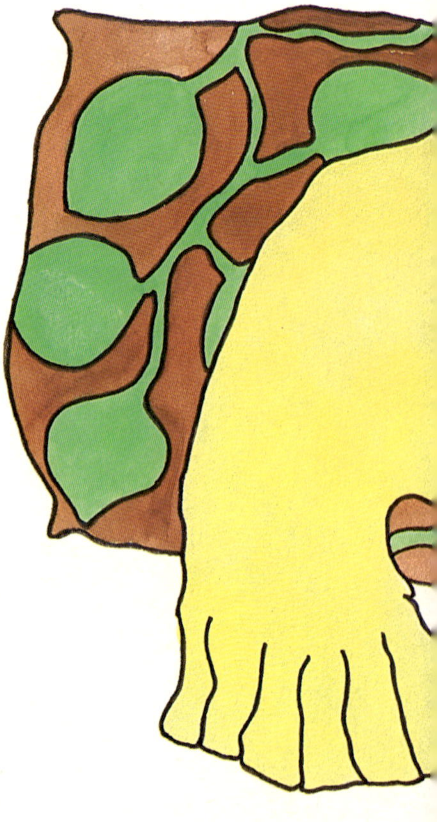

Now that we're being silly,
Let's carry it one step more
What would you say
if a canary
Suddenly started to snore?

What would you think
if you met a bee
That could yodel,
instead of buzz?
Would you think that were
more important
Than what a bee really does?

Oh, what would a banana say
If a banana could really talk?
"I have no bones,
I have no stones,
And I've never learned to walk."

Henry O'Smithers swallowed a clock
And of course it ticked,
When he wanted to talk!
What a predicament, what a stew!
He'd rather tick than talk
It's true.

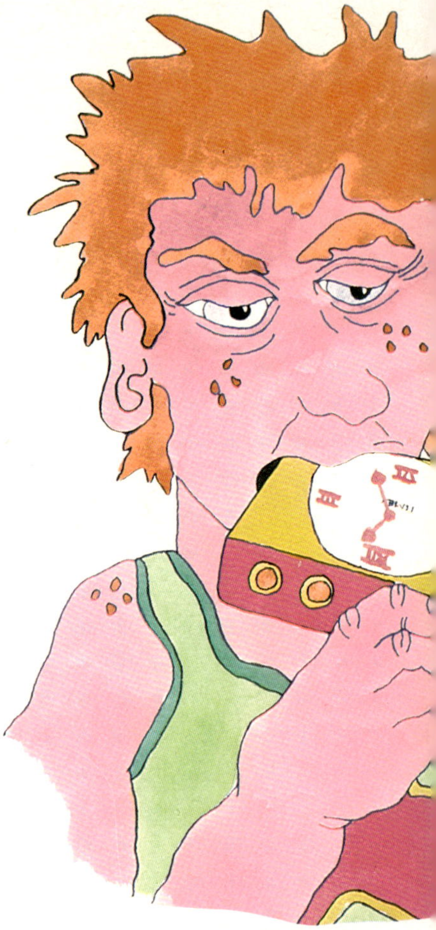

A shoe was gulped by Jenny McComb;
It walked to school and she stayed home.
What a predicament, what a stew!
Imagine being left—
By a wandering shoe!

What would happen if you swallowed a ring?
Would it ding-a-ling if you wanted to sing?
To avoid a predicament, a terrible stew
Be very careful what you chew!

Tick, tick, tock
And ding-a-ling
Come on, join in
And let's all sing.

What a predicament,
What a stew!
Be very careful
What you chew!

Whoops! I was sliding . . . not gracefully gliding
Across a lake of ice.
Whoops! I was sliding . . . not gracefully gliding
And skating, they told me, was nice?

A lion has all that hair
And he can't even fit in a barber's chair!

I saw four dancing
chickens
One, two, three, then four
They tapped their way
to a grocery store
"What do you need?"
And they replied:
(Once they had tapped
their way inside)
"A head of cabbage cut up fine
Some fiddleheads for when we dine.
A bit of this, a ball of string,
And then I guess that's everything.
Oh, wait—four fat dills
from those kegs
And then my dear,
a dozen eggs."

There once was a boy with a very large spoon
Who tried to make cookies the size of the moon
He stirred and stirred, and what do you know?
He fell into the bowl of dough.

When people came, they said
"Bless my soul,
There's a very large raisin
in this bowl
A raisin that speaks
and wears a bow tie,
Enough of a raisin
for raisin pie!"

Then the boy took the spoon,
and bless my soul
He rowed himself
right out of the bowl.

A raisin that rows?
Well bless my soul.

There once was a cat
So nosey and bright
He travelled arounc
In the still of the night
Went sniffing arounc
a big laundry pai
Fell in and starchec
his whiskers and tai
Fell in and starchec
his whiskers and tail

There once was a lady kangaroo,
Who said, "I have a problem or two.
I have a pocket, its part of my skin
My young can hop out
and also hop in.
I want a zipper carefully sewn
So I can be sure I'm hopping alone
So I can be sure I'm hopping alone!"

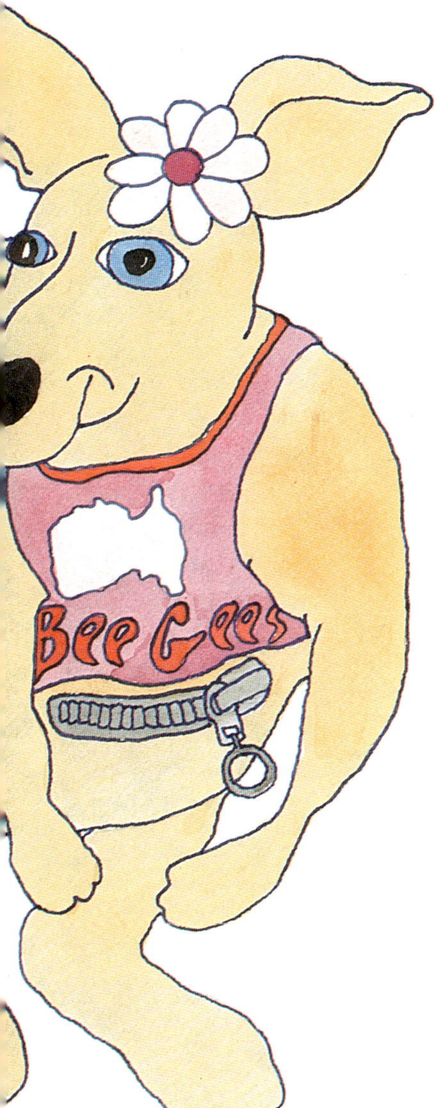

There once was a zebra
With stripes black and white
Really, really a wonderful sight!
And when she got tired of looking just so,
She added more stripes for tic-tac-toe
She added more stripes for tic-tac-toe

JOU
T
NOW PLA
ATTAC
KILLER TO
LAUGHS
GALORE!
THROAT SPECIALISTS
OCTORS

It must be awful to be a giraffe
To have a sore throat
When you want to laugh!

The cat ate my ice cream,
Then climbed up a tree.
I blew soap bubbles,
And they stuck on me.
I don't mind a bit,
When my toe I stub,

BUT . . .
I don't want a
Crocodile in my tub!

City

On a special day you should:
Wink at a monkey
Tango with an eagle
Smile at the kid next door.
But never, never, never
Count the teeth of a lion
When the lion starts to roar!

And:
Waltz with an elephant
Wave at a tiger
Peel a banana, too.
But never, never, never
Swim with an oyster
If the oyster's in a stew!

And: Speak to your turtle
Say "hi" to Myrtle
Invite someone in for tea.
But never, never, never,
Never, never, never
Play tennis with a bee!

A barrel of monkeys
May be lots of fun,
They ate my bananas
One by one.

I don't mind a bit that
My hat fell in the lake,
BUT . . .
A goat on my pillow,
I simply cannot take!

If you hear a knock on your door
Maybe one knock, maybe more
It could be a lion, maybe a bear,
Or two bananas saying,
"Hey, we're a pair."
You may see a reindeer,
Or maybe a moose,
A big flock of chickens,
And one lone goose.

So open the door,
and let them all in.
This looks like a party
About to begin.
A lion, a bear,
Two bananas too,
A reindeer, a moose,
A big flock of chickens,
And one lone goose.

Knock, knock, knock,
Someone's at the door.
Knock, knock, knock,
Wait for one knock more.
You may find a cousin
A friend who lives next door
A cat and a dog,
And that makes four.

Knock, knock, knock,
and one knock more
A zebra and a donkey
Are waiting at the door.
Invite them in
Before they start to run
A zebra and a donkey
Should be lots of fun.

Soon they'll be swinging
Dancing round the chairs
Everybody's happy
And everybody cares
Oh, my goodness
What will you do?
Invite them all in
For a mulligan stew!
A lion, a bear, two bananas, too,
a reindeer, a moose,
some chickens and a goose,
A dog and a cat,
a cousin and a friend,
A zebra and a donkey . . .
well, that's the end!

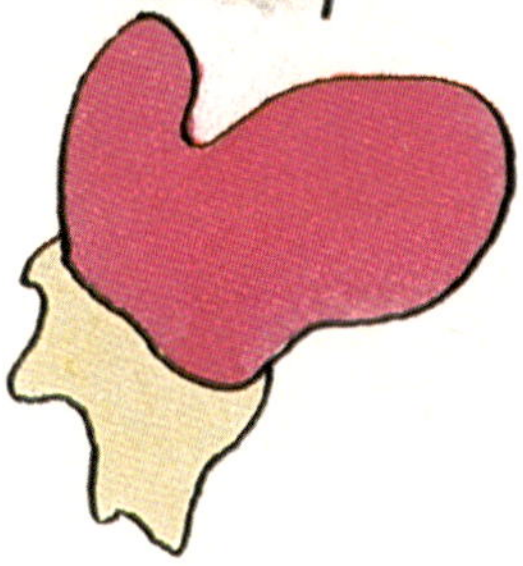

I'm stuck in a snowbank,
What'll I do?
There's frost in my hair,
And snow in my shoe.

I can't move at all,
I'm in so tight,
I may be stuck,
For the long dark night.

This is my problem,
If you want to know,
I can't even wiggle
My big toe

I'll be here forever,
And some cold day,
Someone will come,
And someone will say,

"Hey! Who's that small person, standing there
With a nose of ice, and frosty hair?"

"A statue, I guess, a statue of ice,
A small person statue. Very nice!"

Wait! Before my lips
Both freeze,
I think I'd like to
Give a sneeze!

A. . .A. . .A. . .A
A. . .A. . .Choo!
Wow! What a mighty
sneeze, can do!

I'm me again,
Me that's who!
A. . .A. . .A. . .A
A. . .A. . .Choo!

What would I like to be
If not a person? Let me see,
A waterfall that can never rest?
A jar of honey—Grade A best?
A freckle that is here to stay
And gets bigger on a sunny day?
A fishing tackle with a hook?
A river or a running brook?
A boat with a big white sail?
How about a rusty nail?
A window? Hammer? A buggy, too?
Or a sneeze—a big AAACHOO?
A bump? A pot? A cooking fork?
A shiny bottle with a cork?
A lightning rod? A flower pot?
An exclamation mark? A dot?
A dining table or a chair?
The holey socks I sometimes wear?
No! I guess I'd rather be
A human person, namely ME!
But sometimes, yes, I have a dream
I'm a dish that holds ice cream!